SOOR PLOOMS AND SAIR KNEES

Soor Plooms and Sair Knees

Growing up in Scotland after the War

Written and Illustrated by
BOB DEWAR

BIRLINN

First published in 2010 by
Birlinn Limited
West Newington House
10 Newington Road
Edinburgh
EH9 1QS

www.birlinn.co.uk
2
Text and artwork copyright © Bob Dewar 2010

ISBN: 978 1 84158 862 9

British Library Cataloguing-in-Publication Data
A catalogue record for this book is available from the
British Library

Designed and typeset
by James Hutcheson

Printed and bound
by Gutenberg Press, Malta

Contents

'Haddies'

Introduction

IT WAS A TIME OF IMAGINATION. A time, some say, of charm and innocence. But such comments are always made in retrospect, and I simply I got on with enjoying myself in a Scotland of post-war austerity. Austerity was normal. Being a free-range child was normal. Nae problem.

This was a time of best pals who were called 'best pals', of imaginary cowboys and Indians on the golf course and in the back green. On Saturday mornings we went to film clubs in the local cinema; in the evening we listened to the radio. We ate home-cooked and home-baked foods, year-round comfort foods – a lot of flour, sugar, lard, flaccid tripe, boiled white puddings, Swiss roll and cloutie dumplin' with nicely coagulated custard. We worked it off with the four-times-a-day trek to and from school, playing street games and going for a wee message on behalf of every family in the street.

It was a time of hand-knitted socks held up by a broad elastic garter that made an itchy red hand-knitted sock pattern on your leg. Once a week we went to the cubs and scouts. We'd emerge into a night that smelled of coal fires, a hot threepenny bit digging into our sweaty palms as we headed to the chippie. We built secret dens and 'Tarzie' swings. And we were confused about God and germs because you couldn't see or hear either. My ordinary post-war austerity childhood was happy and perplexed in turn.

At the root of my consternation was the total lack of enlightenment or worthwhile information from any adult. Was it true that some people had a lavatory *inside* their house? Or – this seemed very unlikely – a bath?

What was university? Nobody I knew had gone there. Perhaps the elitist enclave of *Eagle*-comic-reading bairns of the car-owning minority – the doctor, the minister, the heidmaster – might have known about universities. And other local clever folk might also have known,

but they didn't play in the street with us of the underclass who were all headed for the *terra incognita* of grown-upness and the factory, where the rumoured indoor lavatory pans for said clever folk were made. Quite a mystery.

Still, life was rarely dull. There was the interesting ramble to and from school. This included diversions to fascinating places – the coal yard, a visit to the joiner's yard to leap into the sawdust heap, the mart (abattoir) and the factory. The ramble did not include the fruit shop – that had to be avoided at all costs on account of the rumoured deadly banana spider lurking there. One nip from him (or her), it was said, and complete paralysis of one side of the body would follow. There was also the trip to the sweetie shop for a long stare at the penny tray. Gob Stopper, Highland Toffee or liquorice root – decisions were tough.

In school we did a lot of chanting, starting with the times tables every morning. That was after prayers and a small bottle of milk that was usually warm because it was stored beside the huge clanking radiators. If you didn't want to drink the milk, you could amuse yourself by blowing down the regulation school straw rather than sucking. This resulted in a satisfying gurgling noise and a fair amount of bubbles. Teachers were terrifying. They wore black gowns and would stride the corridors shouting, 'You, boy! Hands out of pockets,' trailing the scents of brylcreem and tobacco in their wake. Boys and girls were treated as separate species. They were discouraged from mingling. I spent a lot of time gazing at the girl across the aisle. Not that I lusted after her – the object of my affection was her large, two-tier wooden pencil case, complete with well-sharpened pencils each with a rubber on the end.

After school, I did a lot of staring, and there was plenty of scope for that in my street, with its regular visitors – the rag-and-bone man, the woman who sold pink or whole milk from her dairy cart, the coalman who also had a horse and cart, and Alfie the sweep, who appeared black of face and trundling his equipment in a hand cart. My opinion of these people was gleaned from eavesdropping on adult conversations that I did not wholly understand. Alfie the sweep was rumoured to make a poor job of cleaning chimneys because every time he came by there were fewer and fewer bristles on his brush. I stared at all these people.

When I wasn't staring at people, I was exploring the vast hinterland beyond the last half-built council house. This was another world – arable countryside, the land of pick-your-own

brambles, tattie howking, raspberry picking, woods and fields alive with rabbits. I discovered smallholder family horticulture – women in wrap-around floral aprons and black Wellingtons who made their own butter.

There was the country estate with its run-down big hoose and the self-styled laird. He wore new hand lasted Jermyn Street brogues so we knew he wasn't old money. Old money always wore hand-me-downs. There was his 'gamie' with a twelve-bore who shot and trapped weasels, stoats, rooks and other not obviously edible things. He'd string the carcasses on a gate as a warning to anything around that still had a pulse.

Looking back on my childhood it seems less like another world and more like another planet. Yet at the same time it feels like it all happened days rather than decades ago. The drawings in this book are very much a personal journey into the past, but I hope for many who grew up at the same time they will bring back nostalgic memories, and for others, they will offer an amusing and illuminating glimpse into the way we lived not so very long ago.

BOB DEWAR

The Lone Ranger
Rides Again
(On the Golf Course)

*Childhood Delights
and Diversions*

The local policeman – a figure who inspired fear and panic. You will be arrested; there will be a trial, after which you will be thrown into a small dark cell with only bread and water to eat and drink. You will have to wear an itchy suit covered with little arrows, break rocks with a pick axe and clank, in chains, round and round the exercise yard.

All this for pinching apples from the trees of a more affluent area than the one you lived in. Nobody wanted to eat the apples, of course (they were small, hard and bitter), but as a child it was your job to pinch them so you could stamp on them or throw them at things.

The alarm call would be said in a fake American accent; "Quick! Run for it, men! He's probably armed!" Followed by pelting down the street. You were living briefly in your own movie – later to dread the knock on the door – that never came.

Bob-a-job week (now discontinued) was for cubs and scouts, and meant you got paid one shilling for performing a task and had your job card signed. The one shilling was discretionary and might be more – some people even gave tips. Others took the shilling to be the sum to pay for a tiny uniformed churl or serf to labour at an impossible task. The man in this picture opposite is saying: 'That deid tree is needin' to come down.'

Uniformed youth organizations – boy scouts, guides brownies, wolf cubs – had a combined membership of 2 million in the 1950s. Despite much sniggering at long poles, flappy shorts and woggles now, back then kids loved the whole thing. Scouts were allowed to carry sheath knives; cubs and brownies were unarmed.

Rossi's chip shop, owned by an Original First Generation Italian (not Scoto-Italian, with names like Luigi McNab and Franco McDonald). Cubs squeeze in like a bunch of green grapes. 'Vinegar, laddie!' was not a question but an order – the big, hand-cut chips are doused with vinegar and encrusted with salt in a flamboyant flourish. Chips were eaten on the spot, 3d a poke.

The pinnacle of fine dining was 'sittin' in', the equivalent of eating at The Ivy or the River Café today. Fish and chips were served on a heavy china plate, with a mug of strong tea, sliced bread and stork margarine. High points were control of the condiments and mutual chip counting, including the crispy ones, and saving your favourite chip till last.

Deep in the dingy interior of the newspaper and tobacconist's shop could be glimpsed a flash of colour – comics! Almost too many to list, they featured war heroes, sporting heroes and were all very British. The strips had strict story-line rules – the prankster or the buffoon always got a slapstick comeuppance in the last frame. Girls' comics had a lot of pony strips and also featured cruel uncles, ice skating, plucky 'gels' and ballerinas. Postwar austerity reduced comics to two colours – black and red; black and grey. Quite often the red would smudge on the page and come off on your hands because of the poor paper quality – it was like Izal toilet roll without the shiny side.

The Eagle was rather a superior comic – nice artwork, nice paper – at a superior price: 3d rising to 4½d. Those who could afford it would pore over the latest issue with a knowing smile and then loudly discuss the exploits of Dan Dare, pilot of the future. Those excluded for pecuniary reasons would hover around the exclusive clique, breathing in the rarefied air and trying to sneak a peek.

Swapping American 10-cent action comics featuring heroes such as Superman, Ghost Riders in the Sky, Wonderwoman, Captain Marvel, Tarzan, Flash Gordon was a serious business – the *Canadian Star Weekly* comic section was swappable too, the less virile could keep up with Li'l Abner and Daisy Mae, Bringing Up Father, Pogo, The Katzenjammer Kids, and the rest.

The Lone Ranger calls. The little sister was Tonto, though she disliked answering to that name. 1960s Feminists talked a lot about the 'Tonto Syndrome'.

With only the slightest nod towards witches and ghouls, guisers dressed up in a jumble of old clothes (no bright plastic scream-masks as seen in supermarkets now) before descending on soft-touch relatives or neighbours to treat them to a shrill rendition of 'The Skye Boat Song'. Sometimes songs from the repertoire of Bing Crosby or the Andrews Sisters were weedily belted out on a penny whistle or − even worse − a kazoo.

Guisers were welcomed inside and a tin bath for dookin' for apples was often provided, as were treacle scones hanging from a string. So guisers emerged, soaking wet, face well treacled, clutching a threeppeny bit. The neep for the lantern was softened by gentle boiling, cooled and then carved out − NB carving a raw neep is near impossible, so do not try this at home or you could end up in an Accident and Emergency Unit.

Note the discreet holding out of hands to encourage donation, and burnt cork for moustache and eyebrows on the child who has dressed up to look like Charlie Chaplin

The imaginary horse, called Thunder or Diablo, trained to gallop from nowhere at your, and only your, whistle. You rode like the wind across the rolling plains of the local golf course to right unspecified wrongs. This magnificent stallion also reared into view at the 18th hole at sunset. Silhouetted against a dramatic sky, he stood beside you as you waved your hat at the cheering crowd of grateful townsfolk. Actually the golfers looked unimpressed, obviously unaware of the hoards of scalp-hungry Indians on the fairway you and your trusty steed had seen off.

'Reach for the sky, stranger!' But the strangers are generally unimpressed. Cowboys, and the occasional Indian, were inspired by the ABC cinema Saturday morning children's film club (see p. 29), the ABC minors, which showed cowboy films featuring Roy Rodgers and Trigger, Gabby Hayes, Gene Autry , Lash LaRue and Tom Mix. All cowboys were neat and tidy with leather chaps and lots of fringes. Indians were less well turned-out and rode to jeers of derision mostly because the saddles could be clearly seen under their saddle blankets. For that (and other more heinous crimes) they were slaughtered weekly.

Following the popularity of Harry Houdini, magicians and escape artists performed at local halls everywhere, but magic shows could also be done on a more domestic scale. Dad sent to Gamages, (a famous London magic store) for mail-order tricks – Chinese linking rings, the incredible collapsing magic wand and the disappearing egg in the bag. Tricks were also made by enthusiastic family members. Domestic displays of magic required a long-suffering audience, though children always got thunderous applause and a threepenny bit from kindly-disposed neighbours and relatives.

The 'cartie guider', so called because the vehicle, constructed from soap boxes and pram wheels, could be guided by a rope – a bit of cut-off washing line – tied to a front axle. At least that was the theory. These carties could reach a scary speed – but that was the point. No brakes, or breaks that didn't work, meant your 'good' school shoes were decimated.

'Heiders' involved keeping one eye on the ball and flapping your arms around a lot. The usual made-in-Pakistan leather football was heavy as a cannon ball when wet.

ABC Minors was the Saturday morning film club. Some great films, mostly older ones, like Harold Lloyd in *Safety Last* (1923), Laurel and Hardy in *Leave 'em Laughing* (1928), Willam S. Hurt in *The Gunfighter* (1916), and the Marx Bros in *Duck Soup*, *A Day at the Races* etc. But mostly the standard fare was shorts and cheaply-made cowboy, extravaganzas all in black and white. The big features, like *The African Queen* (1951) and *High Noon* (1952) were shown later in the day.

You might return with a parent on Saturday Night, no age restrictions then. Edward G. Robinson and George Raft films could be enjoyed for the carnage, snappy hats, ties and two-tone shoes.

Conkers in season.

This is a slightly out-of-control skipper.

The secret den and the Tarzie swing. This was not playing 'housies' – this was serious stuff. The den would be defended to the death against those foolish enough not to heed the dire warnings to keep out. Later in life, den-makers would spend a fair amount of time in sheds.

Trains, planes and automobiles. Cars, Matchbox '53, Dinky '50s airfix kits '52 Train Hornby Dublo post-war early version. There were also tin cars from India – sharp round the edges and likely to lacerate fingers.

High tig was a street and playground game. One person was 'it'. Everyone else climbed onto a wall. They'd jump down from the wall, run about and try not to get caught. If caught, they were out of the game. If they escaped the catcher they'd jump back onto the wall and then jump down and run around again. Running about required a lot of shrill screaming (in a good way).

Tadpoles! The promise of metamorphosis hardly ever got beyond the wee-legs stage, particularly if a mother or teacher took exception to the mucky pondwater and replaced it with crystalline tap water, which looked nice and clean but contained no nutrients. Due to threat of 'tadicide', taddies had to be smuggled into the house and kept secret in original pond water.

Learning to swim in the outdoor paddling pool was very popular. It was glamorised of course by Esther Williams, not to mention Busby Berkeley. Movies with formation swimming teams appealed to girls. Hollywood beckoned if you got the hang of the backstroke and perfected the fixed smile. Johnny Weismuller and Lex Barker (two swimming Tarzans), appealed to boys. Wrestling a mighty crocodile would be a doddle if you could swim.

Usually you taught yourself or your little sister to swim in five or six inches of water with floatation device and accessories of your choice: ear plugs, nose clips, goggles and face masks – plenty of clammy rubber.

The snail races. Roman snails or common or garden snails (*Helix Pomatia* and *Helix Aspersa*) were gently placed in the middle of a circle. Snails are speedier than was generally thought, but appeared to have no sense of direction.

Teachers,
Times Tables
and the Tawse
School

The headmaster, or 'heidie'. A nice, if remote, figure who appeared from time to time when staff and children are assembled (but for what reason they were never sure). The children all wondered what he was talking about, and the all-female staff fidgeted discreetly. He is adored by one or two female teachers – OK, OK, just one.

Slow and almost glacial enunciation disguised his local accent, as he peppered his address with moralistic jokes, golf anecdotes and references to people you'd never heard of. The 'jokes' were followed by a private chuckle and a slight rocking movement, and the ticking of the clock.

Seems implausible but true, but when late for school – as children who live nearby often are – this smallholder's son would batter down the three hundred yards of pavement on his half-daft young pony, which would then make the return journey home on his own. Teachers ignored this eccentric form of transport – their authority ending at the school gate.

Children were segregated at the school gate. A muckle brick wall divided the front of the school and the two playgrounds at the back. Furtive attempts at communication – like throwing apple cores over the wall – were the only way to make acquaintance with someone of the opposite sex.

The Tawse, the Belt, the Lochgelly special, the Strap. At some schools, at least, the rumour was that the headmaster had a cauldron of boiling mustard (not water) to make the strap extra nippy. Parents thought this belting was deserved because the teacher knew best. Once, a Tinker boy in our class was belted. The next day his father burst into the classroom and, lifting the teacher off the ground, shook him like a rat – a real Schadenfreude moment. Smug gloating all round and envy to have a dad like that.

Oh happiness! – the school Bakelite big valve radio. The welcome trundle of the school radio trolley along the corridor (decor inspired by Russian mental institutions) which signified special educational programmes. These often featured a small questioning child with uncle tramping through the countryside on the look-out for various types of wildlife – a raven, an avocet, an eagle and other birds you will never see on your back green.

The essential stop on the way to school was the sweetie shop. Life would be strange if you were not to continue the journey without a penny dainty embedded in your teeth or, on a good day, a McCowan's Highland toffee bar. The sweetie shop ladies would slowly drift off with a fixed smile or shift impatiently from foot to foot as you made your choice. But this was a serious consumer decision that required much careful deliberation and could not be taken lightly.

The School Gym – a place of thin, hurtling sweaty figures. Random blasts of the Acme-thunderer whistle were the signal for boys and girls to separate. The gym equipment, always called 'the Apparatus', was heaved from cupboards. The Apparatus included Itchy coconut matting on which somersaults were performed, a wooden vaulting horse (POWs busy tunnelling below), bean bags, more coconut fibre formed into large and heavy medicine balls, benches, rubber rings and ropes. Wall bars were already in place.

This is the peelie-wally wee teacher you will hate for the rest of your life. You want to hunt him down to inflict revenge – set his breeks on fire, perhaps. The casual and indifferent skelp on the head or rattle up the lug, aka damage to the tympanic membrane as teaching aid, apparently never did me any harm. The gratuitous violence employed by teachers could make simple facts like the capital of Scotland or two-times-two drain from your brain.

A routine ticking off, when you discover you are a paltry, worthless nematode. 'You, small boy! Hands out of your pockets. Don't answer back, and none of your dumb insolence either. Small boy, you are an idler; lazy slovenly, a slouch, a sluggardly drone, a laggard, a shirker! With this display of insolence it's clear you'll amount to nothing. Hands out of your pockets or you'll get what for . . . I've got my eye on you.'

Things to pause and stare at on the way to school: the local factory, a dreary concrete building with folk rushing about. What are they doing? How do you make a sink? Home for dinner (at lunch time) – and back to school via another interesting and circuitous route. The factory siren ('The Bummer') sounded at a quarter to two – time to sprint back to the classroom.

SINK AND LAVATORY LTD.

Ca' n' the Mangle

Box Brownie Snapshots of Everyday Life

Slightly more affluent folk who were proud owners of a swanky new TV set were obliged to share certain worthy popular programmes such as those featuring Philip Harben and Marguerite Patten, the first TV chefs, with less fortunate neighbours. So ten or more lady neighbours would sit in a darkened room drinking tea and eating tomato sandwiches gazing at black-and-white cookery demonstrations flickering in the distance.

A rare sight – TV aerial on your lum. Quite a status symbol in those years. Some had an aerial and no TV set, just to incite envy in the neighbours.

The local doctor was almost a local celeb. Here he cuts a dash in his DAKS suit. One stroke of the omnipotent pen could give you a week off work – 'on the seek'. No fool, of course, he was a man to confide in (entre nous). Patients left with a prescription for some analgesic or Glauber's salts (for constipation) – proof there was something really wrong with them and the doctor's time had not been wasted.

Patients were left outside in all weathers, waiting for the surgery to open. It was first come first served; no appointments. Once inside, a ripple of excitement would permeate the waiting room (dark brown lino, never-lit fire and ex-church pews) at the glimpse of the doctor. A sighting of the great man would also bring on a shuffling and loud coughing. (Some families, however, would wait for a light tapping at the door from the Grim Reaper before they bothered the doctor.)

A confusion: God and germs
– two things you can't see or
hear but which are everywhere.
    Germs are about to be
swallowed. Everyone knows
worms are loupin' with germs.
(What is a germ? You can't
hear or see it creeping up or
jumping out at you.)

The Church of Scotland Minister, a respected local figure. This
was a very good job as it provided plenty of tea and sponge cake
with home-made jam assembled from a Zena Skinner or Mabel
Constanduros recipe. Iced fruit slice, Swiss roll and crispy cakes
were also acceptable ecclesiastical fare.

Factory feet, coal dust, cats, blasts of dust-laden air from the street etc. all took their toll on the communal tenement stair. This constant assault on cleanliness engendered fierce scrubbing accompanied by Richter-scale levels of rebuke should you have squeezed past carrying your coal scuttle

Collecting small lumps of coal from the coal trucks at the far end of the railway sidings in the old pram was a common activity. Coal trucks were shunted about a lot and quite a lot of coal fell between the tracks. This was a late evening bit of bare-faced audacity, and a cheap form of entertainment.

The communal stair-heid lavvie served the top two floors (at least in the tenement I lived in), about twelve people in all, and was built onto the outside of the stair tower at the back of the building. Inside there was a large supply of torn newspaper (for obvious purposes but also handy for those keen to catch up on recent events). The lav itself, which stood proudly on a sturdy pedestal, had a mighty wooden seat built to last a thousand years. Everything was so clean you could you could eat your breakfast off the floor (doubtful if this was ever put to the test). Compared with the outside lav on a cold and blustery night, this was paradise.

Tenement lavs for the ground-floor folk were in the back courtyard along with the with coal sheds (similar-looking doors could cause embarrassment). Ladies of the ground floor were seldom seen leaving and entering, but could be heard flapping and scuffling their way in baffies and dressing gown. Torches provided essential illumination.

The rag-and-bone man offered a balloon or a goldfish in exchange for rags and bones. In reality goldfish were seldom, if ever, seen; neither were bones, the average household not having a handy pile of bones at their disposal (but see p. 63). Generally a small, shrivelled unblown-up balloon, rather than the anticipated enormous helium-filled affair, was offered in exchange for your dad's tie. Bitter disappointment and disillusionment were followed by awkward questions as to the location of the missing garment.

Lady residents would titter that Alfie the Sweep was missing a few bristles on his brush, meaning he was short of the full shilling. There was always a fuss prior to his arrival as newspapers were placed all over the floor and furniture. Alfie's workmate (equally encrusted with soot) would sometimes drop a large iron ball down the lum, knocking off soot and bricks from the ledges inside the chimney on its way. The rumour was that the soot was good for the garden, so was kept.

Tinkers, as these travelling people were called, were astute in their judgement. They targeted the more affluent houses and knew all the tricks. Linen was brought from a central warehouse and came machine embroidered. Clothes pegs were hand crafted – split hazel and held at the top by a strip of tin can. Lucky white heather was always thought to be counterfeit.

Bones were collected from the back door of the butcher's shop (blood, fish and bone fertilizer were big at the time). The huge festering heap was removed, leaving only a puzzled community of blue bottles and maggots

This is how my grandmother (Dewar) looked at around eighty-four years old. She lived mostly on porridge, took very long (ten-mile) walks and was a bookie's runner, collecting bets from neighbours who didn't want to be seen entering or leaving the bookmaker's. The neighbours took a punt on the horses – but pretended they didn't.

SOOR PLOOMS AND SAIR KNEES

The coal man arrived to deliver the major fuel of the day wearing steel-toed boots and a studded leather back protector. He heaved the bag onto his back and dumped a couple of bags into the individual coal houses. This was the 'big' coal, although tenement householders would dispute that, shouting 'shale', 'dross', 'wee stuff' to each other once he'd gone They never complained to the coal man himself – he might not come back. The coal man was my hero because he let me ride to the end of the street on the back of his horse.

My grandmother's attic flat had two bedrooms, which she let out to summer visitors and a room with a cooker in it. She lived and slept here. The room had gas mantle, coal fire, bed- table, budgie, gas boiler (lit with a match), armchair, sink radio – what more do you need? The radio ran on an accumulator which was recharged every week at a local garage.

The valve radio or wireless. Fathers would use the 'twiddle tuner' to go 'round the dial' to find radio stations and tune into favourite programmes – *Life with the Lyons* (with Bebe Daniels), *The Billy Cotton Band Show, Music While You Work, Housewives' Choice, Family Favourites, The Brains Trust*. Specifically for kids there were *Children's Hour, Toytown, Larry the Lamb, Mr Growser, Uncle Mac* (Tammie Troot, Brahn the Cat), *Dick Barton, Special Agent,* and *Journey Into Space*. The desired programme would eventually emerge from deafening levels of static and sudden shouts from Oslo and Helsinki as Dad engaged in frantic twiddling.

White sugar in small bags was bought week by week and hoarded for the annual bramble 'jeely' making ritual. It was used to make other kinds of jams too – strawberry, blackcurrant and the unpopular rhubarb and ginger, should by chance some ungrateful people get fed up with the bramble variety.

Judged unfit even to 'ca' the mangle', you'd be packed off to your gran's on wash day with a flask of homemade soup. The soup would be potato and leek and the colour close to no. 13 in the Farrow and Ball paint chart, roughly olive.

Use of the out-door communal wash house and mangle was designated by an inflexible rota. Washing accoutrements included wellies, rubber apron and a large wooden stick for lifting clothes in and out out and stirring tangled garments. The boiler was heated by a coal (what else?) fire underneath.

Tatties were the perks of being a 'tattie howker', and the number of freebies was limited only by weight and storage capacity. Mum's proud of her wee working man, though, and the wee working man is proud that she is proud . . .

A wee business round the doors selling surplus milk pasteurised – straight from the cow – and ladled from the milk can into an enamel jug.

During the war it was common practice to keep hens in your back green. War-time austerity stretched well into the '50s. These hens are Rhode Island Reds (best lay breed). People also kept pullets (small hens). There's a cockerel in the picture, but you don't need one for hens to lay (everyone thinks you do, but you don't).

Very local chip shop – each area, even in small towns, had its own.
Everyone thought theirs was better than all the rest.

Bananas began to make a comeback after the war, but were often regarded with trepidation due to the widespread belief that a huge black, deadly tarantula lurked in every crate. Most fruit shops were like the one shown – gloomy and chaotic, which only added to the grim sense of foreboding felt by those with arachnophobic tendencies.

Potted Heid and Broken Biscuits

Shopping, Austerity Style

Almost everything you might need food-wise, along with paraffin, mouse traps and other fascinating things, could be found in the general grocery shop. Butter was left out overnight, every night, in the butter barrel with butter pats hanging up. Nobody seemed to die from butter poisoning. This was in the distant past before hygiene was discovered. Note the most popular brand names of the day and omnipresent cats.

Early form of 'you shop, we drop'. Messages, including 'a wee sensation under the potatoes' (a quarter bottle of Bells) were delivered to your door by bike.

Going for a 'wee message'. Children were sent with a message line to the network of small local shops by their mothers, their extended family, the neighbours and *their* extended families.

On the way back from the shops with a pan loaf, the soft inside of the bread was slowly consumed, leaving a crusty shell. On arrival the hollow loaf was a surprise both to recipient and loaf eater. No rational explanation has ever been able to explain satisfactorily 'the mystery of the bread-eating trance'.

The very unhygienic butcher's shop, with cooked meat next to raw meat and saw dust on the floor to soak up dripping blood. No hand washing in the front shop and not a lot of chill in the counter area either. I worked in a butcher's at the age of twelve as a message boy. Scrubbing out the fat boiler in the back shop was fun.

The small local garage was strictly a male preserve apart from the part-time lady book-keeper – usually a relative of the owner. Customers wandered about talking intensely to other motoring buffs and mechanics about unladen weights, MacPherson strut suspension and big ends No one was allowed to fill their car with petrol by themselves. The rare lady motorist was treated with amused contempt throughout the tricky fuelling procedure. The award-winning lavatory isn't shown here.

The Wee Hough and Tripe Shop defined indoor dreich. They specialised in hough and tripe and were only slightly busy later in the week when the money was running out. Cold, depressing places, whose owners sniffed a lot and had a defiant bunker mentality whilst accepting their lot as sub-prime shoppers refuge . . .

THE WEE
HOUGH and TRIPE
SHOP

HOUGH

TRIPE

TRIPE

HOUGH

OPEN

Dry Lavvies and Tattie Howking

Life in the Rural Hinterland

The self-styled laird lived in the 'Big Hoose' and was occasionally seen in the town with a car full of dogs (not too often, though, as he was usually 'temporarily out of funds'). He was happiest in the heather-clad moors on the Glorious Twelfth 'bringing income to deprived rural areas'. Part of the country set, he sat on many local committees and stared out the window a lot wearing expensive leather baffies.

The lady laird, adept at hands-on repair and equally at home mending fences and roofs or stripping down a mower or Aga. Sheepskin mitts and pearls were worn at all times.

Gamekeepers learned their trade from their fathers (who had also been gamekeepers on the same estate). Old-fashioned methods predominated, and the ground was littered with all kinds of traps – (wire) rabbit snares, gin (not Gordon's) traps, spring steel taps, wood pigeon cage traps. Gamekeepers also shot at anything that moved. Sometimes dispatched stoats, crows and weasels were hung on a gate in a kind of macabre Scottish Voodoo warning to trespassers, poachers and other stoats, weasels and crows. The gamekeeper would also double as a ghillie if there was a bit of water about on the estate, giving him the chance to slaughter otters and heron as well. Note the gamekeeper's dog of choice – cowed springer spaniel cross. The fear here, as a small boy, was that you would end up hanging upside down on the gate yourself with your hand-knitted woolen underpants exposed for all to see.

SOOR PLOOMS AND SAIR KNEES

Gathering wild brambles to make bramble jelly was a females-in-the-family thing, though small boys were just about tolerated. Groups of womenfolk would bustle out at top speed into the countryside to the 'secret' family bramble bushes, optimistically carrying large baskets and empty biscuit tins. Serious bramble picking then ensued. This was always done with a sense of frenzied urgency, as the secret site might be discovered by strangers, and in minutes the whole place might be swarming with rival pickers. Once all the receptacles were heavy with berries, the intrepid pickers would stagger home, get the big jeely pan down and the muslin bags out. The jeely-making would start right away.

Picking rasps for a farmer. Once the punnets were full, they'd be weighed. You'd climb on a green-with-mould – hefty wooden platform which sat in the berry field year after year. Low murmurs of discontent accompany the punnet-weighing. You'd feel suspicious of the scales: it would have taken forever to pick all these rasps – you must have earned more than that!

To increase the weight of the punnet liquid could
be added.

Farmworkers Big Tam and Wee Tam. These men were out in the field all week in the sun, wind and rain. Whilst their faces turned red, the top half of the foreheads remained pure white on account of their omnipresent bunnets, worn to preserve their Brylcreamed hair for the Saturday night dance.

Tattie howker chic: waiting by the roadside
for the tattie bus. The clothes are in good
part ex-Army, British and Polish mostly.
Everyone had old gas mask satchels to
carry the 'piece'.

The grieve was a man with a big stride. One of his jobs, besides staring round like an unsophisticated Hannibal Lecter, was to pace out the 'bits' (stretches of ground for each tattie picker/howker), which seemed to reach to the horizon. Tatties were put into wire baskets and picked up by the 'bogie' (trailer), which was pulled by a small grey Massey Ferguson tractor driven by a man or woman wrapped in sacks. The man or woman always wore a fixed doomed expression.

SOOR PLOOMS AND SAIR KNEES

Loads of root vegetables – particularly carrots – were grown in allotments. The widespread belief was that Spitfire pilots were fed carrots because it improved the eyesight. Have you ever seen a rabbit wearing specs? was the joke.

'Dig for Victory' and 'Potato Pete' wartime posters urged veg planting, and allotments continued big time in the post-war period. They were a refuge too for Dads, accompanied by chairs, kettles, heaters and other household cast-offs. There is now a waiting list of 80,000 for allotments in the current downturn.

The smallholder's pride and joy – a large black, a breed common at this time (I was nearly trampled by one). This pig is being given treats – neep and tattie peelings, bread and various other unidentifiable foodstuffs. The smallholder's life was not TV's *The Good Life*: they lived in a shabby 'cottar hoose' with a range of self-built ramshackle steadings, some hens, a pig and maybe a goat to milk. I knew one smallholder who even grew tobacco. Eggs, butter and veg were bartered. There were a lot of small-holdings scattered throughout the countryside a couple of miles outside towns but these were eventually swallowed up by urban sprawl. It always seemed like a good life to me.

A sub-prime rural lavatory, late 1940s/early 1950s. This was one on a smallholding owned by two large Polish gents who had elected to stay in Scotland after the war. There were flies (only a few shown here). The two 'CC' marks on the side indicate sub-standard wood (Government approved).

Country children walked miles to and from
school. No row of 'muckle hummers' parked
at the school gate.

Soggy Swimsuits
and Spam Sandwiches

*Holidays at home,
not abroad*

Off on holiday on a Highland branch line. Of course all such lines disappeared thanks to Dr Beeching's callous cuts, making travel in the Highlands formidable for a while.

In contrast to those on a Highland branch line, larger railway stations had staff – friendly porters who trundled your suitcase about on a trolley, a station master who spoke to you. The branch line weighing machine had a long list of instructions. Step on the scale insert, 1d. Chocolate from the choclate machine was twice the price of chocolate from the shop, much like today.

Clammy costumes and the shivery bite. The boy's wearing hand-knitted woollen swimming trunks and the girl's got a ruched swimming costume and a rubber swimming cap. The water retention of the woollen costume was phenomenal – it felt like around a hogshead (12 barrels) of clammy North Sea. As a result 'slippage' could be a problem, and the ability to walk comfortably when wet was severely impaired.

The caravan holiday. Not much
change over the years!

The highlight of the summer holidays was the beach picnic. Spam sandwiches were accompanied by sliced hard-boiled eggs, sliced tomato, lettuce, salad cream and American cream soda. Olive oil was sold only in chemists' shops and was used as sun oil and for cleaning ears. You could get it in wee bottles but you could also take along your own bottle to be filled. Note the tank traps (top left) – big concrete blocks strung along the coast to repel invasion. The excitement of collecting shells, paddling in the sea, collecting crustaceans and building sandcastles kept children entertained whilst mothers read a book, knitted and drank tea freshly boiled on the Primus stove.

Knobbly Knees Contest 7.30 am.

Many went off to one of the well-known and popular holiday camps. They loved being jollied along by the holiday camp jolliers. We might have been poor, but we are also snobs: we didn't go.

A favourite holiday was spent with my family, my best pal and my best pal's family. We stayed in a sparsely furnished remote cottage. There was no telly, no radio – in the evenings we played ludo, cards and word games, mostly the Minister's Cat. In the morning we'd get sent to fetch milk from the nearest farm, which was usually miles away. We shouted, laughed and sang against a backdrop of magnificent scenery, which we barely noticed, being more interested in the sheep, the corbies (hooded crows), farm machinery and dumped rusting cars. It was total freedom. We returned exhausted and happy, just as our parents hoped – particularly the exhausted bit.